ADVAITA VEDANTA

ADVAITA VEDANTA
THE SCIENTIFIC RELIGION

SWAMI VIVEKANANDA

GYAN

Published by

Gyan Publishing House
5, Ansari Road
Daryaganj, New Delhi-110002
Phone: 011-47034999, 9811692060
E-mail: books@gyanbooks.com

Distribution Network
gyanbooks.com
India, USA, Canada, UK, Australia

ISBN: 978-93-6780-983-9 (PB)

First Published, 1952

2nd Impression 2024

Printed at: Gyan Press, Delhi.

ADVAITA VEDANTA
Author: SWAMI VIVEKANANDA

ADVAITA VEDANTA
The Scientific Religion

BY

SWAMI VIVEKANANDA

ADVAITA VEDANTA

The Scientific Religion

(Delivered at Lahore on the 12th Nov., 1897)

Two worlds there are in which we live, one the external, the other, the internal. Human progress has been made, from days of yore, almost in parallel lines along both these worlds. The search began in the external, and man at first wanted to get answers for all the deep problems from outside nature. Man wanted to satisfy his thirst for the beautiful and the sublime from all that surrounded him ; he wanted to express himself and all that was within him in the language of the concrete ; and grand indeed were the answers he got, most marvellous ideas of God and worship, and most rapturous expressions of the beautiful. Sublime ideas came from the external world indeed. But the other, opening out for humanity later, laid out before him a universe yet sublimer, yet more beautiful, and infinitely more expansive. In the Karmakanda portion of the Vedas, we find the most wonderful ideas of religion inculcated, we find the most wonderful ideas about an over-ruling Creator, Preserver and Destroyer of the universe presented before us, in language sometimes the most soul-stirring. Most of you perhaps remember that most wonderful Sloka in the Rig-Veda Samhita where you get the description of chaos, perhaps the sublimest that has ever been attempted yet. In spite of all this, we find it is only a painting of the sublime outside, we find that yet it is gross, that something of matter yet clings to it. Yet we find that it is only the expression of the Infinite in the language of matter, in the language of the finite, it is the infinite of the muscles and not of the mind; it is the infinite of space, and not of thought. Therefore in the second portion or Jnana-kanda, we find there is altogether a different procedure. The first was a search in external nature for the truths of the universe; it was an attempt to get the solution of the deep problems of life from the material world. **यस्यैते हिमवन्तो महित्वा**— "Whose glory these Himalayas declare." This is a grand idea, but yet it was not grand enough for India. The Indian mind had to fall back, and the research took a different direction altogether, from the external the search came to the internal, from matter to mind. There arose the cry, "When a man dies, what becomes of him?" यस्तीत्येके नायमस्तीति चैके &c. "Some say that he exists, others, that he is gone; say, O king of Death, what is the truth?" An entirely different procedure we find here. The Indian mind got all that could be had from the external world, but it did not feel satisfied with that; it wanted to search further, to dive into its own soul, and the final answer came.

The Upanishads, or the Vedanta, or the Aranyakas, or Rahasya, is the name of this portion of the Vedas. Here we find at once that religion has got rid of all external formalities. Here we find at once that spiritual things are told not in the language of matter, but in the language of the spirit, the superfine, in the language of the superfine. No more any grossness attaches to it, no more is there any compromise with things of worldly concern. Bold, brave, beyond the conception of the present day, stand the giant minds of the sages of the Upanishads, declaring the noblest truths that have ever been preached to humanity, without any compromise, without any fear. This, my countrymen, I want to lay before you. Even the Jnana-kanda of the Vedas is a vast ocean; many lives are necessary to understand even a little of it. Truly has it been said of the Upanishads by Ramanuja, that they form the head, the shoulders, the crest of the Vedas, and surely enough the Upanishads have become the Bible of modern India. The Hindus have the greatest respect for the Karma-kanda of the Vedas, but, for all practical purposes, we know that for ages by Sruti has been meant the Upanishads, and the Upanishads alone. We know that all our great philosophers, whether Vyasa, Patanjali or Gautama, and even the father of all philosophy, the great Kapila himself, whenever they wanted an authority for what they wrote, everyone of them found it in the Upanishads, and nowhere else, for therein are the truths that remain for ever.

There are truths that are true only in a certain line, in a certain direction, under certain circumstances, and for certain times, those that are founded on the institutions of the times. There are other truths which are based on the nature of man himself, and which must endure so long as man himself endures. These are the truths that alone can be universal, and in spite of all the changes that have come to India, as to our social surroundings, our methods of dress, our manner of eating, our modes of worship,—these universal truths of the Srutis, the marvellous Vedantic ideas, stand out in their own sublimity, immovable, unvanquishable, deathless, and immortal. Yet the germs of all the ideas that were developed in the Upanishads had been taught already in the Karma-kanda. The idea of the cosmos, which all sects of Vedantists had to take for granted, the psychology which has formed the common basis of all the Indian schools of thought, had there been worked out already and presented before the world. A few words, therefore, about the Karma-kanda are necessary before we begin the spiritual portion, the Vedanta; and first of all I should like to explain the sense in which I use the word Vedanta.

Unfortunately there is the mistaken notion in modern India, that the word Vedanta has reference only to the Advaita system, but you must always remember that in modern India, the three Prasthanas are considered equally important in the study of all the systems of religion. First of all there are the Revelations, the Srutis, by which I mean the Upanishads. Secondly, among our philosophies, the Sutras of Vyasa have the greatest prominence, on account of their being the consummation of all the preceding systems of philosophy. These systems are not contradictory to one another, but one is based on another, and there is a gradual unfolding of the theme which culminates in the Sutras of Vyasa. Then, between the Upanishads and the Sutras, which are the systematising of the marvellous truths of the Vedanta, comes in Sri Gita, the divine commentary of the Vedanta. The Upanishads, the Vyasa Sutras, and the Gita, therefore, have been taken up by every sect in India that wants to claim authority for orthodoxy, whether Dualist, or Visishtadvaitist, or Advaitist ; the authorities of each of these are the three Prasthanas. We find that a Sankaracharya, or a Ramanuja, or a Madhwacharya, or a Vallabhacharya, or a Chaitanya,—any one who wanted to propound a new sect—had to take up these three systems and write only a new commentary on them. Therefore it would be wrong to confine the word Vedanta only to one system, which has arisen out of the Upanishads. All these are covered by the word Vedanta. The Visishtadvaitist has as much right to be called a Vedantist as the Advaitist; in fact I will go a little further and say that what we really mean by the word Hindu is really the same as Vedantist. I want you to note, that these three systems have been current in India almost from time immemorial—for you must not believe that Sankara was the inventor of the Advaita system; it existed ages before Sankara was born; he was one of its last representatives. So with the Visishtadvaita system; it had existed ages before Ramanuja appeared, as we already know from the commentaries he has written; so with the Dualistic systems that have existed side by side with the others. And with my little knowledge, I have come to the conclusion that they do not contradict each other. Just as in the case of the six Darshanas, we find they are a gradual unfolding of the grand principles, whose music beginning far back in the soft low notes, ends in the triumphant blast of the Advaita, so also in these three systems we find the gradual working up of the human mind towards higher and higher ideals, till everything is merged in that wonderful unity which is reached in the Advaita system. Therefore these three are not contradictory. On the other hand I am bound to tell you, that this has been a mistake committed by not a few. We find that an Advaitist teacher keeps intact those texts which especially teach Advaitism, and tries to interpret the Dualistic or Qualified-non-dualistic texts into his own meaning. Similarly we find Dualistic teachers trying to read their Dualistic meaning into Advaitic texts. Our Gurus were great men, yet there is a saying, "Even the faults of a Guru must be told." I am of opinion that in this only they were mistaken. We need not go into text-torturing, we need not go into any sort of religious dishonesty, we need not go into any sort of grammatical twaddle, we need not go about trying to put our own ideas into texts which were never meant for them, but the work is plain and becomes easier, once you understand the marvellous doctrine of Adhikarabheda.

It is true that the Upanishads have this one theme before them कस्मिन्नु भगवो विज्ञाते सर्वमिदं विज्ञातं भवति—What is that knowing which we know everything else ?" In modern language, the theme of the Upanishads is to find an ultimate unity of things. Knowledge is nothing but finding unity in the midst of diversity. Every science is based upon this ; all human knowledge is based upon the finding of unity in the midst of diversity ; and if it is the task of small fragments of human knowledge, which we call our sciences, to find unity in the midst of a few different phenomena, the task becomes stupendous when the theme before us is to find unity in the midst of this marvellously diversified universe, where prevail unnumbered differences in name and form, in matter and spirit,—each thought differing from every other thought, each form differing from every other form. Yet, to harmonise these many planes and unending Lokas, in the midst of this infinite variety to find unity, is the theme of the Upanishads. On the other hand, the old idea of Arundhati Nyaya applies. To show a man the fine star Arundhati, one takes the big and brilliant star nearest to it, upon which he is asked to fix his eyes first, and then it becomes quite easy to direct his sight to Arundhati. This is the task before us, and to prove my idea I have simply to show you the Upanishads, and you will see it. Nearly every chapter begins with Dualistic teaching, Upasana. God is first taught as some one who is the Creator of this universe, its Preserver, and unto whom everything goes at last. He is one to be worshipped, the Ruler, the Guide of nature, external and internal, yet appearing as if He were outside of nature and external. One step further, and we find the same teacher teaching that this God is not outside of nature, but immanent in nature. And at last both ideas are discarded, and whatever is real is He; there is no difference. तत्त्वमसि श्वेतकेतो—"Svetaketu, That thou art." That Immanent One is at last declared to be the same that is in the human soul. Here is no compromise; here is no fear of others' opinions. Truth, bold truth, has been taught in bold language, and we need not fear to preach the truth in the same bold language to-day, and, by the grace of God, I hope at least to be the one who dares to be that bold preacher.

To go back to our preliminaries. There are first two things to be understood,—one, the psychological aspect common to all the Vedantic schools, and the other, the cosmological aspect. I will first take up the latter. To-day we find wonderful discoveries of modern science coming upon us like bolts from the blue, opening our eyes to marvels we never dreamt of. But many of these are only re-discoveries of what had been found ages ago. It was only the other day that modern science found that even in the midst of the variety of forces there is unity. It has just discovered that what it calls heat, magnetism, electricity, and so forth, are all convertible into one unit force, and as such, it expresses all these by one name, whatever you may choose to call it. But this has been done even in the Samhita ; old and ancient as it is, in it we meet with this very idea of force I was referring to. All the forces, whether you call them gravitation, or attraction, or repulsion, whether expressing themselves as heat, or electricity, or magnetism, are nothing but the variations of that unit energy. Whether they express themselves as thought, reflected from Antahkarana, the inner organs of man, or as action from an external organ, the unit from which they spring is what is called the Prana. Again, what is Prana? Prana is Spandana or vibration. When all this universe shall have resolved back into its primal state, what becomes of this infinite force? Do they think that it becomes extinct? Of course not. If it became extinct, what would be the cause of the next wave, because the motion is going in wave forms, rising, falling, rising again, falling again? Here is the word Srishti, which expresses the universe. Mark that the word does not mean creation. I am helpless in talking English; I have to translate the Sanskrit words as best as I can. It is Srishti, projection. At the end of a cycle, everything becomes finer and finer and is resolved back into the primal state from which it sprang, and there it remains for a time, quiescent, ready to spring forth again. That is Srishti, projection. And what becomes of all these forces, the Pranas? They are resolved back into the primal Prana, and this Prana becomes almost motionless—not entirely motionless,—and that is what is described in the Vedic Sukta. "It vibrated without vibrations"—Anidavatam. There are many technical phrases in the Upanishads difficult to understand. For instance, take this word Vata; many times it means air and many times motion, and often people confuse one with the other. We must guard against that. And what becomes of what you call matter? The forces permeate all matter; they all dissolve into Akasha, from which they again come out; this Akasha is the primal matter. Whether you translate it as ether, or anything else, the idea is that this Akasha is the primal form of matter. This Akasha vibrates under the action of Prana, and when the next Srishti is coming up, as the vibration becomes quicker, the Akasha is lashed into all these wave forms which we call suns, and moons, and systems.

We read again :—**यदिदं किंच जगत् सर्वं प्राण एजति निःसृतम्।** Everything in this universe has been projected, Prana vibrating." You must mark the word Ejati, because it comes from Eja, to vibrate, Nihsritam projected, Yadidam Kincha—whatever in this universe.

This is a part of the cosmological side. There are many details working into it. For instance, how the process takes place, how there is first ether, and how from the ether come other things, how that ether begins to vibrate, and from that Vayu comes. But the one idea is here, that it is from the finer that the grosser has come. Gross matter is the last to emerge and the most external, and this gross matter had the finer matter before it. Yet we see that the whole thing has been resolved into two, but there is not yet a final unity. There is the unity of force, Prana; there is the unity of matter called Akasha. Is there any unity to be found among them again? Can they be melted into one? Our modern science is mute here, it has not yet found its way out; and if it is doing so, just as it has been slowly finding the same old Prana and the same ancient Akasha, it will have to move along the same lines. The next unity is the omnipresent impersonal Being known by its old mythological name as Brahma, the four-headed Brahma, and psychologically called Mahat. This is where the two unite. What is called your mind is only a bit of this Mahat caught in the trap of the brain, and the sum total of all minds caught in the meshes of brains is what you call Samashti, the aggregate, the universal. Analysis had to go further; it was not yet complete. Here we are each one of us, as it were, a microcosm, and the world taken altogether is the macrocosm. But whatever is in the Vyasti, the particular, we may safely conjecture that a similar thing is happening also outside. If we had the power to analyse our own minds we might safely conjecture that the same thing is happening in the cosmic mind. What is this mind is the question. In modern times in Western countries, as physical science is making rapid progress, as physiology is step by step conquering stronghold after stronghold of old religions, the Western people do not know where to stand, because to their great despair, modern physiology at every step has identified the mind with the brain. But we in India have known that always. That is the first proposition the Hindu boy learns, that the mind is matter, only finer. The body is gross, and behind the body is what we call the Sukshma Sharira, the fine body or mind. This is also material, only finer ; and it is not the Atman. I will not translate this word to you in English, because the idea does not exist in Europe ; it is untranslatable. The modern attempt of German philosophers is to translate the word Atman by the word 'Self,' and until that word is universally accepted it is impossible to use it. So, call it as Self or anything, it is our Atman. This Atman is the real man behind. It is the Atman that uses the material mind as its instrument, its Antahkarana, as is the psychological term for the mind. And the mind by means of a series of internal organs works the visible organs of the body. What is this mind ? It was only the other day that Western philosophers have come to know that the eyes are not the real organs of vision, but that behind these are other organs, the Indriyas, and if these are destroyed, a man may have a thousand eyes, like Indra, but there will be no sight for him. Aye, your philosophy starts with this assumption, that by vision is not meant the external vision. The real vision belongs to the internal organs, the brain centres inside. You may call them what you like, but it is not that the Indriyas are the eyes, or the nose, or the ears. And the sum total of all these Indriyas plus the Manas, Buddhi, Chitta, Ahamkara, &c., is what is called the mind, and if the modern physiologist comes to tell you that the brain is what is called the mind, and that the brain is formed of so many organs, you need not be afraid at all; tell him that your philosophers knew it always; it is one of the very first principles of your religion.

Well then, we have to understand now what is meant by this Manas, Buddhi, Chitta, Ahamkara, etc. First of all, let us take Chitta; it is the mind-stuff,—a part of the Mahat—it is the generic name for the mind itself, including all its various states. Suppose on a summer evening, there is a lake, smooth and calm, without a ripple on its surface. And suppose some one throws a stone into this lake. What happens? First there is the action, the blow given to the water; next, the water rises and sends a reaction towards the stone, and that reaction takes the form of a wave. First the water vibrates a little, and immediately sends back a reaction in the form of a wave. The Chitta let us compare to this lake, and the external objects are like the stones thrown into it. As soon as it comes in contact with any external object by means of these Indriyas—the Indriyas must be there to carry these external objects inside—there is a vibration, what is called the Manas, indecisive. Next there is a reaction, the determinative faculty, Buddhi, and along with this Buddhi flashes the idea of Aham and the external object. Suppose there is a mosquito sitting upon my hand. This sensation is carried to my Chitta and it vibrates a little ; this is the psychological Manas. Then there is a reaction, and immediately comes the idea that I have a mosquito on my hand, and that I shall have to drive it off. Thus these stones are thrown into the lake, but in the case of the lake every blow that comes to it is from the external world, while in the case of the lake of the mind, the blows may either come from the external world, or the internal world. This whole series is what is called the Antahkarana. Along with it, you ought to understand one thing more that will help us in understanding the Advaita system later on. It is this. All of you must have seen pearls and most of you know how pearls are formed. A grain of sand enters into the shell of a pearl oyster, and sets up an irritation there, and the oyster's body reacts towards the irritation and covers the little particle with its own juice. That crystallises and forms the pearl. So the whole universe is like that, it is the pearl which is being formed by us. What we get from the external world is simply the blow. Even to be conscious of that blow we have to react, and as soon as we react, we really project a portion of our own mind towards the blow, and when we come to know of it, it is really our own mind as it has been shaped by the blow. Therefore, it is clear even to those who want to believe in a hard and fast realism of an external world, which they cannot but admit in these days of physiology,—that supposing we represent the external world by "X," what we really know is "X" plus mind, and this mind-element is so great that it has covered the whole of that "X," which has remained unknown and unknowable throughout, and therefore, if there is an external world it is always unknown and unknowable. What we know of it is as it is moulded, formed, fashioned by our own mind. So with the internal world. The same applies to our own soul, the Atman. In order to know the Atman we shall have to know It through the mind, and therefore what little we know of this Atman is simply the Atman plus the mind. That is to say, the Atman covered over, fashioned, and moulded by the mind, and nothing more. We shall return to this a little later, but we will remember what has been told here.

The next thing to understand is this. The question arose, that this body is the name of one continuous stream of matter; every moment we are adding material to it, and every moment material is being thrown off by it, like a river continually flowing, vast masses of water always changing places; yet all the same, we take up the whole thing in imagination, and call it the same river. What do we call the river? Every moment the water is changing, the shore is changing, every moment the environment is changing; what is the river then ? It is the name of this series of changes. So with the mind. That is the great Kshanika Vijnana Vada doctrine, most difficult to understand, but most rigorously and logically worked out in the Buddhistic philosophy, and this arose in India in opposition to some part of the Vedanta. That had to be answered and we shall see how, later on, it could only be answered by Advaitism and by nothing else. We will see also how, in spite of people's curious notions about Advaitism, people's fright about Advaitism, it is the salvation of the world, because therein alone is to be found the reason of things. Dualism and other *isms* are very good as means of worship, very satisfying to the mind, and may be, they have helped the mind onward ; but if man wants to be rational and religious at the same time, Advaita is the one system in the world for him. Well now, we shall regard the mind as a similar river, continually filling itself at one end, and emptying itself at the other end. Where is that unity which we call the Atman? The idea is this, that in spite of this continuous change in the body, and in spite of this continuous change in the mind, there is in us something that is unchangeable, which makes our ideas of things appear unchangeable. When rays of light coming from different quarters fall upon a screen, or a wall, or upon something that is not changeable, then and then alone it is possible for them to form a unity, then and then alone it is possible for them to form one complete whole. Where is this unity in the human organs, falling upon which, as it were, the various ideas will come to unity and become one complete whole? This certainly cannot be the mind itself, seeing that it also changes. Therefore there must be something which is neither the body nor the mind, something which changes not, something permanent, upon which all our ideas, our sensations fall to form a unity, and a complete whole, and this is the real soul, the Atman, of man. And seeing that everything material, whether you call it fine matter, or mind, must be changeful, seeing that what you call gross matter, the external world, must also be changeful in comparison to that,—this unchangeable something, cannot be of material substance, therefore it is spiritual, that is to say, it is not matter ; it is indestructible, unchangeable.

Next will come another question—apart from those old arguments which only rise in the external world, the arguments in support of Design—who created this external world, who created matter, &c. ? The idea here is to know truth only from the inner nature of man, and the question arises just in the same way as it arose about the soul. Taking for granted that there is a soul, unchangeable, in each man, which is neither the mind, nor the body, there is still a unity of idea among the souls, a unity of feeling, of sympathy. How is it possible that my soul can act upon your soul, where is the medium through which it can work, where is the medium through which it can act ? How is it I can feel anything about your souls ? What is it that is in touch both with your soul, and with my soul ? Therefore there is a metaphysical necessity of admitting another soul, for it must be a soul which acts in contact with all the different souls, and in and through matter ; one Soul which covers and interpenetrates all the infinite number of souls in the world, in and through which they live, in and through which they sympathise, and love, and work for one another. And this universal Soul is Paramatman, the Lord God of the universe. Again, it follows that because the Soul is not made of matter, since It is spiritual, It cannot obey the laws of matter, It cannot be judged by the laws of matter. It is therefore unconquerable, birthless, deathless and changeless.

नैनं छिन्दन्ति शस्त्राणि नैनं दहति पावकः ।
नचैनं क्लेदयंत्यापो न शोषयति मारुतः ॥
नित्यः सर्वगतः स्थाणुरचलोऽयं सनातनः ॥

"This Self weapons cannot pierce, nor fire can burn, water cannot wet nor air can dry up. Changeless, all-pervading, unmoving, immovable, eternal is this Self of man." We learn according to the Gita and the Vedanta, that this individual Self is also Vibhu, and according to Kapila, is omnipresent. Of course there are sects in India which hold that the Self is Anu, infinitely small; but what they mean is Anu in manifestation; its real nature is Vibhu, all-pervading.

There comes another idea, startling perhaps, yet a characteristically Indian idea, and if there is any idea that is common to all our sects, it is this. Therefore I beg you to pay attention to this one idea and to remember it, for this is the very foundation of everything that we have in India. The idea is this. You have heard of the doctrine of physical evolution preached in the Western world by the German and the English savants. It tells us that the bodies of the different animals are really one, the differences that we see are but different expressions of the same series, that from the lowest worm to the highest and the most saintly man it is but one, the one changing into the other, and so on, going up and up, higher and higher, until it attains perfection. We had that idea also. Declares our Yogi Patanjali— जात्यन्तरपरिणामः प्रकृत्यापूरात् । One species—the Jati is species—changes into another species—evolution ; Parinama means one thing changing into another, just as one species changes into another. Where do we differ from the Europeans ? Patanjali says, Prakrityapurat—"By the infilling of nature."

The European says, it is competition, natural and sexual selection, &c., that forces one body to take the form of another. But here is another idea, a still better analysis, going deeper into the thing, and saying—"By the infilling of nature." What is meant by this infilling of nature? We admit that the amœba goes higher and higher until it becomes a Buddha; we admit that, but we are, at the same time, as much certain that you cannot get an amount of work out of a machine unless you have put it in in some shape or other. The sum total of the energy remains the same, whatever the forms it may take. If you want a mass of energy at one end you have got to put it in at the other end, it may be in another form, but the amount of energy that should be produced out of it must be the same. Therefore, if a Buddha is the one end of the change, the very amœba must have been the Buddha also. If the Buddha is the evolved amœba, the amœba was the involved Buddha also. If this universe is the manifestation of an almost infinite amount of energy, when this universe was in a state of Pralaya, it must have represented the same amount of involved energy. It cannot have been otherwise. As such it follows that every soul is infinite. From the lowest worm that crawls under our feet to the noblest and greatest saints, all have this infinite power, infinite purity, and infinite everything. Only the difference is in the degree of manifestation. The worm is only manifesting just a little bit of that energy; you have manifested more, another god-man has manifested still more; that is all the difference. But that infinite power is there all the same. Says Patanjali :—ततः क्षेत्रिकवत् । "Like the peasant irrigating his field." Through a little corner of his field he brings water from a reservoir somewhere, and perhaps he has got a little lock that prevents the water from rushing into his field. When he wants water he has simply to open the lock, and in rushes the water of its own power. The power has not to be added, it is already there in the reservoir. So every one of us, every being, has as his own background such a reservoir of strength, infinite power, infinite purity, infinite bliss, and existence infinite,—

only these locks, these bodies, are hindering us from expressing what we really are to the fullest.

And as these bodies become more and more finely organised, as the Tamoguna becomes the Rajoguna, and as the Rajoguna becomes Sattvaguna, more and more of this power and purity becomes manifest, and therefore it is that our people have been so careful about eating and drinking, and the food question. It may be that the original ideas have been lost, just as with our marriage —which, though not belonging to the subject, I may take as an example. If I have another opportunity I will talk to you about these ; but let me tell you now that the ideas behind our marriage system are the only ideas through which there can be a real civilisation. There cannot be anything else. If a man or a woman were allowed the freedom to take up any woman or man as wife or husband, if individual pleasure, if satisfaction of animal instincts, were to be allowed to run loose in society, the result must be evil, evil children, wicked and demoniacal. Aye, man in every country is, on the one hand, producing these brutal children, and on the other hand multiplying the police force to keep these brutes down. The question is not how to destroy evil that way, but how to prevent the very birth of evil, and so long as you live in society your marriage certainly affects every member of it; and therefore society has the right to dictate whom you shall marry, and whom you shall not. And great ideas of this kind have been behind the system of marriage here; what they call the astrological Jati of the bride and bridegroom. And in passing I may remark, that according to Manu a child who is born of lust is not an Aryan. The child whose very conception and whose death is according to the rules of the Vedas, such is an Aryan. Yes, and less of these Aryan children are being produced in every country, and the result is the mass of evil which we call Kali Yuga. But we have lost all these ideals; it is true we cannot carry all these ideas to the fullest length now, it is perfectly true we have made almost a caricature of some of these great ideas. It is lamentably true that the fathers and mothers are not what they were in old times, neither is society so educated as it used to be, neither has society that love for individuals that it used to have. But, however faulty the working out may be, the principle is sound; and if its application has become defective, if one method has failed, take up the principle and work it out better; why kill the principle? The same applies to the food question; the work and details are bad, very bad indeed, but that does not hurt the principle. The principle is eternal and must be there. Work it out afresh, and make a reformed application.

This is the great idea of the Atman which every one of our sects in India has to believe. Only, as we shall find, the Dualists preach that this Atman by evil works becomes Sankuchita, *i.e.,* all its powers and its nature become contracted, and by good works again that nature expands. And the Advaitist says, that the Atman never expands nor contracts, but seems to do so. It appears to have become contracted. That is all the difference, but all have the one idea that our Atman has all the powers already, not that anything will come to It from outside, not that anything will drop into It from the skies. Mark you, your Vedas are not inspired, but expired, not that they came from anywhere outside, but they are the eternal laws living in every soul. The Vedas are in the soul of the ant, in the soul of the god. The ant has only to evolve and get the body of a sage or a Rishi, and the Vedas will come out, eternal laws expressing themselves. This is the one great idea to understand, that our power is already ours, our salvation is already within us. Say either that it has become contracted, or say that it has been covered with the veil of Maya, it matters little ; the idea is there already ; you must have to believe in that, believe in the possibility of everybody—even in the lowest man there is the same possibility as in the Buddha. This is the doctrine of the Atman.

But now comes a tremendous fight. Here are the Buddhists, who equally analyse the body into a material stream and as equally analyse the mind into another. And as for this Atman they state that It is unnecessary ; so we need not assume the Atman at all. What use of a substance, and qualities adhering to the substance ? We say, Gunas, qualities, and qualities alone. It is illogical to assume two causes where one will explain the whole thing. And the fight went on, and all the theories which held the doctrine of substance were thrown to the ground by the Buddhists. There was a break-up all along the line of those who held on to the doctrine of substance and qualities, that you have a soul, and I have a soul, and everyone has a soul separate from the mind and body, and that each one is an individual. So far we have seen that the idea of Dualism is all right; for there is the body, there is then the fine body—the mind, there is this Atman, and in and through all the Atmans, is that Paramatman, God. The difficulty is here, that this Atman and Paramatman are both called substance, to which the mind and body and so-called substances adhere like so many qualities. Nobody has ever seen a substance, none can ever conceive; what is the use of the thinking of this substance? Why not become a Kshanikavadin, and say that whatever exists is this succession of mental currents and nothing more? They do not adhere to each other, they do not form a unit, one is chasing the other, like waves in the ocean, never complete, never forming one unit-whole. Man is a succession of waves, and when one goes away it generates another, and the cessation of these wave-forms is what is called Nirvana. You see that Dualism is mute before this; it is impossible that it can bring up any argument, and the Dualistic God also cannot be retained here. The idea of a God that is omnipresent, and yet is a Person who creates without hands, and moves without feet, and so on, and who has created the universe as a Kumbhakara (potter) creates a Ghata (pot), the Buddhist declares, is childish, and that if this is God, he is going to fight this God and not worship it. This universe is full of misery; if it is the work of a God, we are going to fight this God. And secondly, this God is illogical and impossible, as all of you are aware. We need not go into the defects of the 'design' theory, as all our Kshanikas have shown them full well; and so this Personal God fell to pieces.

Truth, and nothing but truth, is the watchword of the Advaitist. **सत्यमेव जयते नानृतं। सत्येनैव पन्था विततो देवयानः**—"Truth alone triumphs, and not untruth. Through truth alone the way to Devayana lies." Everybody marches forward under that banner; aye, but it is only to crush the weaker man's position by his own. You come with your Dualistic idea of God to pick a quarrel with a poor man who is worshipping an image, and you think you are wonderfully rational, you can confound him, but if he turns round and shatters your own Personal God, and calls that an imaginary ideal, where are you? You fall back on faith and so on, or raise the cry of Atheism, the old cry of a weak man—whosoever defeats him is an atheist. If you are to be rational, be rational all along the line, and if not, allow others the same privilege which you ask for yourselves. How can you prove the existence of this God? On the other hand it can be almost disproved. There is not a shadow of a proof as to His existence, and there are very strong arguments to the contrary. How will you prove His existence, with your God, and His Gunas, and an infinite number of souls which are substance, and each soul an individual? In what are you an individual? You are not as a body, for you know to-day better than even the Buddhists of old knew, that what may have been matter in the sun has just now become matter in you, and will go out and become matter in the plants; then where is your individuality, Mr. so and so? The same applies to the mind. Where is your individuality? You have one thought to-night and another to-morrow. You do not think the same way as you thought when you were a child, and old men do not think the same way as they did when they were young. Where is your individuality then? Do not say it is in consciousness, this Ahamkara, because this only covers a small part of your existence. While I am talking to you, all my organs are working and I am not conscious of it. If consciousness is the proof of existence they do not exist then, because I am not conscious of them. Where are you then with your Personal God theories? How can you prove such a God? Again, the Buddhists will stand up and declare—not only is it illogical, but immoral, for it teaches man to be a coward and to seek assistance outside, and nobody can give him such help. Here is the universe, man made it; why then depend on an imaginary being outside, whom nobody ever saw or felt, or got help from? Why then do you make cowards of yourselves, and teach your children that the highest state of man is to be like a dog, and go crawling before this imaginary being, saying that you are weak and impure, and that you are everything vile in this universe? On the other hand, the Buddhists may urge not only that you tell a lie, but that you bring a tremendous amount of evil upon your children, for, mark you, this world is one of hypnotisation. Whatever you tell yourself that you become. Almost the first words the great Buddha uttered were—"What you think, that you are, what you will think, that you will be." If this is true, do not teach yourself that you are nothing, aye, that you cannot do anything unless you are helped by somebody who does not live here, but sits above the clouds. The result will be that you will be more and more weakened every day; by constantly repeating, "We are very impure, Lord, make us pure," the result will be that you will hypnotise yourselves into all sorts of vices. Aye, the

Buddhists say that ninety per cent. of these vices that you see in every society are on account of this idea of a Personal God; this is an awful idea of the human being that the end and aim of this expression of life, this wonderful expression of life, is to become like a dog. Says the Buddhist to the Vaishnava, "If your ideal, your aim and goal is to go to the place called Vaikuntha where God lives, and there stand before Him with folded hands all through eternity, it is better to commit suicide than do that." The Buddhists may even urge, that that is why he is going to create annihilation, Nirvana, to escape this. I am putting these ideas before you as a Buddhist just for the time being, because nowadays all these Advaitic ideas are said to make you immoral, and I am trying to tell you how the other side looks. Let us face both sides boldly and bravely.

We have seen first of all that this cannot be proved, this idea of a Personal God creating the world; is there any child that can believe this to-day? Because a Kumbhakara creates a Ghata, therefore a God created the world! If this is so, then your Kumbhakara is God also, and if any one tells you that he acts without head and hands you may take him to a lunatic asylum. Has ever your Personal God, the Creator of the world, to whom you cry all your life, helped you,—is the next challenge from modern science. They will prove that any help you have had could have been got by your own exertions, and better still, you need not have spent your energy in that crying, you could have done it better without that weeping and crying. And we have seen that along with this idea of a Personal God comes tyranny and priestcraft. Tyranny and priestcraft have prevailed wherever this idea existed, and until the lie is knocked on the head, say the Buddhists, tyranny will not cease. So long as man thinks he has to cower before a supernatural being, so long there will be priests to claim rights and privileges and to make men cower before them, while these poor men will continue to ask some priest to act as interceder for them. You may do away with the Brahmana, but mark me, that those who do so will put themselves in his place, and will be worse, because the Brahmana has a certain amount of generosity in him, but these upstarts are always the worst of tyrannisers. If a beggar gets wealth, he thinks the whole world is a bit of straw. So these priests there must be, so long as this Personal God idea persists, and it will be impossible to think of any great morality in society. Priestcraft and tyranny go hand in hand. Why was it invented? Because some strong men in old times got people into their hands and said, you must obey us or we will destroy you. That was the long and short of it. महद्भयं वज्रमुद्यतम्। It is the idea of the thunderer, who kills everyone who does not obey him.

Next the Buddhist says, you have been perfectly rational up to this point, that everything is the result of the law of Kārma. You believe in an infinity of souls, and that souls are without birth or death, and this infinity of souls and the belief in the law of Karma are perfectly logical, no doubt. There cannot be a cause without an effect, the present must have had its cause in the past, and will have its effect in the future. The Hindu says Karma is Jada (inert) and not Chaitanya (spirit), therefore some Chaitanya is necessary to bring this cause to fruition. Is it so, that Chaitanya is necessary to bring the plant to fruition ? If I plant the seed and add water, no Chaitanya is necessary. You may say there was some original Chaitanya there, but the souls themselves were the Chaitanya, nothing else is necessary. If human souls have it too, what necessity is there for a God, as say the Jains, who, unlike the Buddhists, believe in souls, and do not believe in God. Where are you logical, where are you moral ? And when you criticise Advaitism and fear that it will make for immorality, just read a little of what has been done in India by Dualistic sects. If there have been twenty thousand Advaitist blackguards, there have also been twenty thousand Dvaitist blackguards. Generally speaking, there will be more Dvaitist blackguards, because it takes a better type of mind to understand Advaitism, and Advaitists can scarcely be frightened into anything. What remains for you Hindus, then ? There is no help for you out of the clutches of the Buddhists. You may quote the Vedas, but he does not believe in them. He will say, "My Tripitakas say otherwise, and they are without beginning or end, not even written by Buddha, for Buddha says he is only reciting them; they are eternal." And he adds, "Yours are wrong, ours are the true Vedas, yours are manufactured by the Brahmana priests, therefore out with them." How do you escape?

Here is the way to get out. Take up the first objection, the metaphysical one, that substance and qualities are different. Says the Advaitist, they are not. There is no difference between substance and qualities. You know the old illustration, how the rope is taken for the snake, and when you see the snake you do not see the rope at all, the rope has vanished. Dividing the thing into substance and quality, is a metaphysical something in the brains of philosophers, for never can they be in effect outside. You see qualities if you are an ordinary man, and substance if you are a great Yogi, but you never see both at the same time. So, Buddhists, your quarrel about substance and qualities has been but a miscalculation which does not stand in fact. But, if substance is unqualified, there can only be one. If you take qualities off from the soul, and show that these qualities are in the mind, really superimposed on the soul, then there can never be two souls, for it is qualification that makes the difference between one soul and another. How do you know that one soul is different from the other ? Owing to certain differentiating marks, certain qualities. And where qualities do not exist how can there be differentiation ? Therefore there are not two souls, there is but One, and your Paramatman is unnecessary, it is this very soul. That One is called Paramatman, that very One is called Jivatman, and so on ; and you Dualists, such as the Sankhyas and others, who say that the soul is Vibhu, omnipresent, how can you make two infinites ? There can be only one. What else ? This One is the one Infinite Atman, everything else is Its manifestation. There the Buddhist stops, but there it does not end. The Advaitist position is not merely a weak one of criticism. The Advaitist criticises others when they come too near him, and just throws them away, that is all, but he propounds his own position. He is the only one that criticises and does not stop with criticism and showing books. Here you are. You say the universe is a thing of continuous motion. In Vyashti (the finite) everything is moving, you are moving, the table is moving, motion everywhere; it is Samsara, continuous motion; it is Jagat. Therefore there cannot be an individuality in this Jagat, because individuality means that which does not change; there cannot be any changeful individuality, it is a contradiction in terms. There is no such thing as individuality in this little world of ours, the Jagat. Thought and feeling, mind and body, men and animals and plants are in a continuous state of flux. But suppose you take the universe as a unit whole; can it change or move? Certainly not. Motion is possible in comparison with something which is a little less in motion, or entirely motionless. The universe as a whole, therefore, is motionless, unchangeable. You are, therefore, an individual then and then alone, when you are the whole of it, when the realisation of "I am the universe" comes. That is why the Vedantist says that so long as there are two, fear does not cease. It is only when one does not see another, does not feel another, when it is all one,—then alone fear ceases, then alone death vanishes, then alone Samsara vanishes. Advaita teaches us therefore that man is individual in being universal, and not in being particular. You are immortal only when you are the whole. You are fearless and deathless only when you are the universe; and then, that which you call the universe is the same as that you call God, the same that you call existence, the same that you call the whole. It is the one undivided Existence which is taken to be the manifold world which we see, as also others who are in the same state of mind as we. People who have done a little better Karma and get a better state of mind, when they die, look upon it as Svarga, and see Indras and so forth. People still higher will see it, the very same thing, as Brahma Loka, and the perfect ones will neither see the earth nor the heavens, nor any Loka at all. This universe will have vanished, and Brahman will be in its stead.

Can we know this Brahman? I have told you of the painting of the Infinite in the Samhita. Here we shall find another side shown, the infinite internal. That was the infinite of the muscles. Here we shall have the Infinite of thought. There the Infinite was attempted to be painted in language positive; here that language failed and the attempt has been to paint it in language negative. Here is this universe, and even admitting that it is Brahman, can we know it? No! No! You must understand this one thing again very clearly. Again and again this doubt will come to you, if this is Brahman, how can we know it? विज्ञातारमरे केन विजानीयात्, "By what can the knower be known?" How can the knower be known? The eyes see everything; can they see themselves? They cannot. The very fact of knowledge is a degradation. Children of the Aryas, you must remember this, for herein lies a big story. All the Western temptations that come to you, have their metaphysical basis on that one thing—there is nothing higher than sense-knowledge. In the East, we say in our Vedas that this knowledge is lower than the thing itself, because it is always a limitation. When you want to know a thing, it immediately becomes limited by your mind. They say, refer back to that instance of the oyster making a pearl and see how knowledge is limitation, gathering a thing, bringing it into consciousness, and to knowing it as a whole. This is true about all knowledge, and can it be less so about the Infinite ? Can you thus limit Him who is the substance of all knowledge, Him who is the Sakshi, the Witness, without whom you cannot have any knowledge, Him who has no qualities, who is the Witness of the whole universe, the Witness in our own souls ? How can you know Him ? By what means can you bind Him up ? Everything, the whole universe, is such a false attempt. This Infinite Atman is, as it were, trying to see His own face, and all, from the lowest animals to the highest of gods, are like so many mirrors to reflect Himself in, and He is taking up still others, finding them insufficient, until in the human body He comes to know that it is the finite of the finite, all is finite, there cannot be any expression of the Infinite in the finite. Then comes the retrograde march, and this is what is called renunciation, Vairagyam.

Back from the senses, back! Do not go to the senses, is the watchword of Vairagyam. This is the watchword of all morality, this is the watchword of all well-being; for you must remember that with us the universe begins in Tapasya, in renunciation; and as you go back and back, all the forms are being manifested before you, and they are left aside one after the other until you remain what you really are. This is Moksha, or liberation.

This idea we have to understand, विज्ञातारमरे केन विजानीयात्,—"How to know the knower?" The knower cannot be known, because if it were known it will not be the knower. If you look at your eyes in a mirror, the reflection is no more your eyes, but something else, only a reflection. Then if this Soul, this Universal, Infinite Being which you are, is only a witness, what good is it? It cannot live, and move about, and enjoy the world, as we do. People cannot understand how the witness can enjoy. "Oh," they say, "you Hindus have become quiescent, and good for nothing, through this doctrine that you are witnesses!" First of all, it is only the witness that can enjoy. If there is a wrestling match, who enjoys it, those who take part in it, or those who are looking on, the outsiders? The more and more you are the witness of anything in life, the more you enjoy it. And this is Anandam, and therefore infinite bliss can only be yours when you have become the witness of this universe, then alone you are a Mukta Purusha. It is the witness alone that can work without any desire, without any idea of going to heaven, without any idea of blame, without any idea of praise. The witness alone enjoys, and none else.

Coming to the moral aspect, there is one thing between the metaphysical and the moral aspect of Advaitism; it is the theory of Maya. Everyone of these points in the Advaita system requires years to understand and months to explain. Therefore you will excuse me if I only just touch them *en passant*. This theory of Maya has been the most difficult thing to understand in all ages. Let me tell you in a few words that it is surely no theory, it is the combination of the three ideas Desha-kala-nimitta—space, time and causation—and this time and space and cause have been further reduced into Nama Rupa. Suppose there is a wave in the ocean. The wave is distinct from the ocean only in its form and name, and this form and this name cannot have any separate existence from the wave; they exist only with the wave. The wave may subside, but the same amount of water remains, even if the name and form that were on the wave vanish for ever. So this Maya is what makes the difference between me and you, between all animals and man, between gods and men. In fact, it is this Maya that causes the Atman to be caught, as it were, in so many millions of beings, and these are distinguishable only through name and form. If you leave it alone, let name and form go, all this variety vanishes for ever, and you are what you really are. This is Maya. It is again no theory, but a statement of facts. When the realist states that this table exists, what he means is, that this table has an independent existence of its own, that it does not depend on the existence of anything else in the universe, and if this whole universe be destroyed and annihilated this table will remain just as it is now. A little thought will show you that it cannot be so. Everything here in the sense-world is dependent and inter-dependent, relative and co-relative, the existence of one depending on the other. There are three steps, therefore, in our knowledge of things; the first is, that each thing is individual, and separate from every other; and the next step is to find that there is a relation and co-relation between all things; and the third is that there is only one thing which we see as many. The first idea of God with the ignorant is that this God is somewhere outside the universe, that is to say, the conception of God is extremely human; He does just what a man does, only on a bigger and higher scale. And we have seen how that idea of God is proved in a few words to be unreasonable and insufficient. And the next idea is the idea of a power we see manifested everywhere. This is the real Personal God we get in the *Chandi*, but, mark me, not a God that you make the reservoir of all good qualities only. You cannot have two Gods, God and Satan; you must have only one, and dare to call Him good and bad, have only one, and take the logical consequences. We read in the *Chandi*—"We salute Thee, O Divine Mother, who lives in every being as peace. We salute Thee, O Divine Mother, who lives in all beings as purity." At the same time we must take the whole consequence of calling Him the All-formed. "All this bliss, O Gargi, wherever there is bliss there is a portion of the Divine." You may use it how you like. In this light before me, you may give a poor man a hundred rupees, and another man may forge your name, but the light will be the same for both. This is the second stage; and the third is that God is neither outside nature nor inside nature, but God and nature and soul and universe are all convertible terms. You never see two things; it is your metaphysical words that have deluded you. You assume that you are a body and have a soul, and that you are both together. How can that be? Try in your own mind. If there is a Yogi among you, he knows himself as Chaitanya, for him the body has vanished. An ordinary man thinks of himself as a body; the idea of spirit has vanished from him; but because the metaphysical ideas exist that man has a body and a soul and all these things, you think they are all simultaneously there. One thing at a time. Do not talk of God when you see matter; you see the effect and the effect alone, and the cause you cannot see, and the moment you can see the cause the effect will have vanished. Where is this world then, and who has taken it off?

"One that is present always as consciousness, the bliss absolute, beyond all bounds, beyond all compare, beyond all qualities, ever-free, limitless as the sky, without parts, the absolute, the perfect,—such a Brahman, O sage, O learned one, shines in the heart of the Jnanin, in Samadhi."

"Where all the changes of Nature cease for ever, who is thought beyond all thoughts, who is equal to all yet having no equal, immeasurable, whom the Vedas declare, who is the essence in what we call our existence, the perfect,—such a Brahman, O sage, O learned one, shines in the heart of the Jnanin in Samadhi."

"Beyond all birth and death, the Infinite One, incomparable, like the whole universe deluged in water in Mahapralaya,—water above, water beneath, water on all sides, and on the face of that water not a wave, not a ripple,—silent and calm, all visions have died out, all fights and quarrels and the war of fools and saints have ceased for ever;—such a Brahman, O sage, O learned one, shines in the heart of the Jnanin in Samadhi."

That also comes, and when that comes the world has vanished.

We have seen then, that this Brahman, this Reality is unknown and unknowable, not in the sense of the agnostic, but because to know Him would be a blasphemy, because you are He already. We have also seen that this Brahman is not this table and yet is this table. Take off the name and form, and whatever is reality is He. He is the reality in everything.

"Thou art the woman, thou the man, thou art the boy, and the girl as well, thou the old man supportest thyself on a stick, thou art all in all in the Universe." That is the theme of Advaitism. A few words more. Herein lies, we find, the explanation of the essence of things. We have seen how here alone we can take a firm stand against all the onrush of logic and scientific knowledge. Here at last reason has a firm foundation, and, at the same time, the Indian Vedantist does not curse the preceding steps; he looks back and he blesses them, and he knows that they were true, only wrongly perceived, and wrongly stated. They were the same truth, only seen through the glass of Maya, distorted it may be,—yet truth, and nothing but truth. The same God whom the ignorant man saw outside nature, the same whom the little-knowing man saw as interpenetrating the universe, and the same whom the sage realises as his own self, as the whole universe itself,—all are One and the same Being, the same entity seen from different standpoints, seen through different glasses of Maya, perceived by different minds, and all the difference was caused by that. Not only so, but one view must lead to the other. What is the difference between science and common knowledge? Go out into the streets in the dark, and if something unusual is happening there, ask one of the passers-by, what is the cause of it. It is ten to one that he will tell you it is a ghost causing the phenomenon. He is always going after ghosts and spirits outside, because it is the nature of ignorance to seek for causes outside of effects. If a stone falls it has been thrown by a devil or a ghost, says the ignorant man, but the scientific man says it is the law of nature, the law of gravitation.

What is the fight between science and religion everywhere? Religions are encumbered with such a mass of explanations which come from outside—one angel is in charge of the sun, another of the moon, and so on *ad infinitum*; every change is caused by a spirit, the one common point of agreement being that they are all outside the thing; while science means that the cause of a thing is sought out by the nature of the thing itself. As step by step science is progressing it has taken the explanation of natural phenomena out of the hands of spirits and angels. Because Advaitism has done likewise in spiritual matters, it is the most scientific religion. This universe has not been created by any extra-cosmic God, nor is it the work of any outside genius. It is self-creating, self-dissolving, self-manifesting, One Infinite

Existence, the Brahman. Tattvamasi Svetaketo—"That Thou art, O Svetaketu!" Thus you see that this, and this alone, and none else, can be the only scientific religion. And with all the prattle about science that is going on daily at the present time in modern half-educated India, with all the talk about rationalism and reason that I hear every day, I expect that whole sects of you will come over and dare to be Advaitists. and dare to preach it to the world in the words of Buddha, बहुजनहिताय बहुजनसुखाय—"for the good of many, for the happiness of many." If you do not, I take you for cowards. If you cannot get over your cowardice, if your fear is your excuse, allow the same liberty to others, do not try to break up the poor idol-worshipper, do not call him a devil, do not go about preaching to every man that does not agree entirely with you; know first, that you are cowards yourselves, and if society frightens you, if your own superstitions of the past frighten you so much, how much more will these superstitions frighten and bind down those who are ignorant? That is the Advaita position. Have mercy on others. Would to God that the whole world were Advaitists to-morrow, not only in theory, but in realisation ! But if that cannot be, let us do the next best thing ; let us take the ignorant by the hand, lead them always step by step just as they can go, and know that every step in all religious growth in India has been progressive. It is not from bad to good, but from good to better.

Something more has to be told about the moral relation. Our boys blithely talk nowadays, they learn from somebody—the Lord knows from whom—that Advaita makes people immoral, because if we are all one and all God, what need of morality will there be at all ! In the first place, that is the argument of the brute, who can only be kept down by the whip. If you are such brutes commit suicide, rather than pass for human beings, who have to be kept down by the whip. If the whip is taken away you will all be demons ! You ought all to be killed, if such is the case ; there is no help for you ; you must always be living under this whip and rod, and there is no salvation, no escape for you.

In the second place, Advaita and Advaita alone explains morality. Every religion preaches that the essence of all morality is to do good to others. And why ? Be unselfish. And why should I ? Some God has said it ? He is not for me. Some texts have declared it ? Let them ; that is nothing to me ; let them all tell it. And if they do, what is it to me ? Each one for himself, and somebody take the hindermost ; that is all the morality in the world, at least with many. What is the reason that I should be moral ? You cannot explain it except when you come to know the truth as given in the Gita—"He, who sees everyone in himself, and himself in everyone, thus seeing the same God living in all, he, the sage no more kills the Self by the self." Know through Advaita that whomsoever you hurt, you hurt yourself ; they are all you. Whether you know it or not, through all hands you work, through all feet you move, you are the king enjoying in the palace, you are the beggar leading that miserable existence in the street ; you are in the ignorant as well as in the learned, you are in the man who is weak, and you are in the strong; know this and be sympathetic. And that is why we must not hurt others. That is why I do not even care whether I have to starve, because there will be millions of mouths eating at the same time, and they are all mine. Therefore I should not care what becomes of me and mine, for the whole universe is mine, I am enjoying all the bliss at the same time; and who can kill me, or the universe? Herein is morality. Here, in Advaita alone, is morality explained. The others teach it, but cannot give you its reason. Then, so far about explanation.

What is the gain? It is strength. Take off that veil of hypnotism which you have cast upon the world, send not out thoughts and words of weakness unto humanity. Know that all sins and all evils can be summed up in that one word, weakness. It is weakness that is the motive power in all evil doing; it is weakness that is the source of all selfishness; it is weakness that makes men injure others; it is weakness that makes them manifest what they are not in reality. Let them all know what they are; let them repeat day and night what they are. Soham.

Let them suck it in with their mothers' milk, this idea of strength—I am He, I am He. This is to be heard first. श्रोतव्यो मन्तव्यो निदिध्यासितव्यः etc. And then let them think of it, and out of that thought, out of that heart will proceed works such as the world has never seen. What has to be done ? Aye, this Advaita is said by some to be impracticable ; that is to say, it is not yet manifesting itself on the material plane. To a certain extent that is true, for, remember the saying of the Vedas—

ओमित्येकाक्षरं ब्रह्म ओमित्येकाक्षरं परम् ।
ओमित्येकाक्षरं ज्ञात्वा यो यदिच्छति तस्य तत् ॥

"Om, this is the Brahman ; Om, this is the greatest reality ; he who knows the secret of this Om, whatever he desires that he gets." Aye, therefore first know the secret of this Om, that you are the Om ; know the secret of this Tattvamasi, and then and then alone whatever you want shall come to you. If you want to be great materially, believe that you are so. I may be a little bubble, and you may be a wave mountain-high, but know that for both of us the infinite ocean is the background, the infinite Brahman is our magazine of power and strength, and we can draw as much as we like, both of us, I the bubble and you the mountain-high wave. Believe therefore in yourselves. The secret of Advaita is—Believe in yourselves first, and then believe in anything else. In the history of the world, you will find that only those nations that have believed in themselves have become great and strong. In the history of each nation, you will always find that only those individuals who have believed in themselves have become great and strong. Here, to India, came an Englishman who was only a clerk, and for want of funds and other reasons he twice tried to blow his brains out, and when he failed, he believed in himself, he believed that he was born to do great things, and that man became Lord Clive, the founder of the Empire. If he had believed the Padris and gone crawling all his life—"Oh Lord, I am weak, and I am low"—where would he have been? In a lunatic asylum. You also are made lunatics by these evil teachings. I have seen all the world over, the bad effects of these weak teachings of humility destroying the human race. Our children are brought up in this way, and is it a wonder that they become semi-lunatics?

This is teaching on the practical side. Believe, therefore, in yourselves, and if you want material wealth, work it out; it will come to you. If you want to be intellectual, work it out on the intellectual plane, and intellectual giants you shall be. And if you want to attain to freedom, work it out on the spiritual plane, and free you shall be, and shall enter into Nirvana, the Eternal Bliss. But one defect which lay in the Advaita was its being worked out so long on the spiritual plane only, and nowhere else; now the time has come when you have to make it practical. It shall no more be a Rahasya, a secret, it shall no more live with monks in caves and forests, and in the Himalayas; it must come down to the daily, everyday life of the people, it shall be worked out in the palace of the king, in the cave of the recluse, it shall be worked out in the cottage of the poor, by the beggar in the street, everywhere, anywhere it can be worked out. Therefore do not fear whether you are a woman or a Sudra, for this religion is so great, says Lord Krishna, that even a little of it, brings a great amount of good. Therefore, children of the Aryas, do not sit idle ; awake, arise, and stop not till the goal is reached. The time has come when this Advaita is to be worked out practically. Let us bring it down from heaven unto the earth ; this is the present dispensation. Aye, the voices of our fore-fathers of old are telling us to bring it down from heaven to the earth. Let your teachings permeate the world, till they have entered into every pore of society, till they have become the common property of everybody, till they have become part and parcel of our lives, till they have entered into our veins and tingle with every drop of blood there.

Aye, you may be astonished to hear, that as practical Vedantists the Americans are better than we are. I used to stand on the sea-shore at New York, and look at the emigrants coming from different countries, crushed, down-trodden, hopeless, unable to look a man in the face, with a little bundle of clothes as all their possession, and these all in rags; if they saw a policeman they were afraid and tried to get to the other side of the footpath. And, mark you, in six months those very men were walking erect, well-clothed, looking everybody in the face; and what made this wonderful difference? Say, this man comes from Armenia, or somewhere else where he was crushed down beyond all recognition, where everybody told him he was a born slave, and born to remain in a low state all his life, and where at the least move on his part he was trodden upon. There everything told him, as it were, "Slave! you are a slave, remain so. Hopeless you were born, hopeless you must remain." Even the very air murmured round him, as it were, "There is no hope for you, hopeless and a slave you must remain;" while the strong man crushed the life out of him. And when he landed in the streets of New York, he found a gentleman, well-dressed, shaking him by the hand; it made no difference that the one was in rags and the other well-clad. He went a step further and saw a restaurant, that there were gentlemen dining at a table, and he was asked to take a seat at the corner of the same table.

He went about, and found a new life, that there was a place where he was a man among men. Perhaps he went to Washington, shook hands with the President of the United States, and perhaps there he saw men coming from distant villages, peasants, and ill-clad, all shaking hands with the President. Then the veil of Maya slipped away from him. He is Brahman, he who has been hypnotised into slavery and weakness, is once more awake, and he rises up and finds himself a man, in a world of men. Aye, in this country of ours, the very birthplace of the Vedanta, our masses have been hypnotised for ages into that state. To touch them is pollution ; to sit with them is pollution ! Hopeless they were born ; hopeless they must remain ! And the result is that they have been sinking, sinking, sinking, and have come to the last stage to which a human being can come. For what country is there in the world where man has to sleep with the cattle ? And for this, blame nobody else, do not commit the mistake of the ignorant. The effect is here and the cause is here too. We are to blame. Stand up, be bold, and take the blame on your own shoulders. Do not go about throwing mud at others; for all the faults you suffer from, you are the sole and only cause.

Young men of Lahore, understand this, therefore, this great sin, hereditary and national, is on our shoulders. There is no hope for us. You may make thousands of societies, twenty thousand political assemblages, fifty thousand institutions. These will be of no use until there is that sympathy, that love, that heart, that thinks for all; until Buddha's heart comes once more into India, until the words of Lord Krishna are brought to their practical use, there is no hope for us. You go on imitating the Europeans and their societies and their assemblages, but let me tell you a story, a fact that I saw with my own eyes. A company of Burmans was taken over to London by some persons here, who turned out to be Eurasians. They exhibited these people in London, took all the money, and then took these Burmans over to the Continent, and left them there for good or evil. These poor people did not know a word of any European language, but the English Consul in Austria sent them over to London.

They were helpless in London, without knowing any one. But an English lady got to know of them, took these foreigners from Burma into her own house, gave them her own clothes, her bed, and everything, and then sent the news to the papers. And, mark you, the next day the whole nation was, as it were, roused. Money poured in and these people were helped out and sent back to Burma. On this sort of sympathy are based all their political and other institutions; it is the rock-foundation of love, for themselves at least. They may not love the world; and the Burmans may be their enemies, but in England, it goes without saying, there is this great love for their own people, for truth and justice and charity to the stranger at the door. I should be the most ungrateful man if I did not tell you how wonderfully and how hospitably I was received in every country in the West. Where is the heart here to build upon? No sooner do we start a little joint-stock company than we try to cheat each other, and the whole thing comes down with a crash. You talk of imitating the English, and building up as big a nation as they are. But where are the foundations? Ours are only sand, and therefore the building comes down with a crash in no time.

Therefore, young men of Lahore, raise once more that mighty banner of Advaita, for on no other ground can you have that wonderful love, until you see that the same Lord is present everywhere. Unfurl that banner of love! "Arise, awake and stop not till the goal is reached." Arise, arise once more, for nothing can be done without renunciation. If you want to help others, your little self must go. In the words of the Christians—you cannot serve God and Mammon at the same time. Have Vairagyam—your ancestors gave up the world for doing great things. At the present time there are men who give up the world to help their own salvation. Throw away everything, even your own salvation, and go and help others. Aye, you are always talking bold words, but here is practical Vedanta before you. Give up this little life of yours. What matters it if you die of starvation, you and I and thousands like us, so long as this nation lives? The nation is sinking, the curse of unnumbered millions is on our heads;—those to whom we have been giving ditch-water to drink when they have been dying of thirst and while the perennial river of water was flowing past; the unnumbered millions whom we have allowed to starve in sight of plenty; the unnumbered millions to whom we have talked of Advaita and whom we have hated with all our strength; the unnumbered millions for whom we have invented the doctrine of Lokachara (usage);—to whom we have talked theoretically that we are all the same and all are one with the same Lord, without even an ounce of practice. "Yet, my friends, it must be only in the mind and never in practice!" Wipe off this blot. "Arise and awake." What matters it if this little life goes; everyone has to die, the saint or the sinner, the rich or the poor. The body never remains for anyone. Arise and awake and be perfectly sincere. Our insincerity in India is awful; what we want is character, that steadiness and character that make a man cling on to a thing like grim death.

"Let the sages blame or let them praise, let Lakshmi come to-day or let her go away, let death come just now, or in a hundred years; he indeed is the sage who does not make one false step from the right path." Arise and awake, for the time is passing and all our energies will be frittered away in vain talking. Arise and awake, let minor things, and quarrels over little details, and fights over little doctrines be thrown aside, for here is the greatest of all works, here are the sinking millions. When the Mohammedans first came into India, what a great number of Hindus were here; but mark, how to-day they have dwindled down. Every day they will become less and less till they wholly disappear. Let them disappear, but with them will disappear the marvellous ideas, of which, with all their defects and all their misrepresentations, they still stand as representatives. And with them will disappear this marvellous Advaita, the crest-jewel of all spiritual thought. Therefore, arise, awake, with your hands stretched out to protect the spirituality of the world. And first of all, work it out for your own country. What we want is, not so much spirituality as a little of the bringing down of the Advaita into the material world. First bread and then religion. We stuff them too much with religion, when the poor fellows have been starving. No dogmas will satisfy the cravings of hunger. There are two curses here, first our weakness, secondly, our hatred, our dried-up hearts. You may talk doctrines by the millions, you may have sects by the hundreds of millions; aye, but it is nothing until you have the heart to feel; feel for them as your Veda teaches you, till you find they are parts of your own bodies, till you realise that you and they, the poor and the rich, the saint and the sinner, are all parts of One Infinite Whole, which you call Brahman.

Gentlemen, I have tried to place before you a few of the most brilliant points of the Advaita system, and now the time has come when it should be carried out into practice, not only in this country but everywhere. Modern Science and its sledge-hammer blows are pulverising the porcelain foundations of all Dualistic religions everywhere. Not only here are the Dualists torturing texts till they will extend no longer,—for texts are not India-rubber,—it is not only here that they are trying to get into the nooks and corners to protect themselves, it is still more so in Europe and America. And even there something of this idea will have to go from India. It has already got there. It will have to grow and increase, and save their civilisations too. For, in the West, the old order of things is vanishing, giving way to a new order of things, which is the worship of gold, the worship of Mammon. Thus, this old crude system of religion was better than the modern system, namely,—competition and gold. No nation, however strong, can stand on such foundations, and the history of the world tells us that all that had such foundations are dead and gone. In the first place we have to stop the in-coming of such a wave in India. Therefore, preach the Advaita to every one, so that religion may withstand the shock of modern science. Not only so, you will have to help others; your thought will help out Europe and America. But above all, let me once more remind you that here is need of practical work, and the first part of that is, that you should go to the sinking millions of India, and take them by the hand remembering the words of the Lord Krishna:

इहैव तैर्जितः सर्गो येषां साम्ये स्थितं मनः ।
निर्दोषं हि समं ब्रह्म तस्मात् ब्रह्मणि ते स्थिताः ॥

"Even in this life they have conquered relative existence whose minds are firm-fixed on the sameness of everything, for God is pure and the same to all; therefore, such are said to be living in God."